I Remember:
Chicago Veterans of War

Published by Big Shoulders Books
DePaul University
Chicago, Illinois

Second Edition

ISBN: 978-0-692-48510-1
Library of Congress Control Number: 2015947059

Cover photograph: Laszlo Kondor, *Chicago Flag, Viet Nam, 1971.*
Copyright © Laszlo Kondor Collection, Courtesy of National Veterans Art Museum

Big Shoulders Books logo design by Robert Soltys

I Remember: Chicago Veterans of War

EDITED BY CHRIS GREEN // FOREWORD BY JIM FAIRHALL

ABOUT BIG SHOULDERS BOOKS

Big Shoulders Books aims to produce one book each year that engages intimately with the Chicago community and, in the process, gives graduate students in DePaul University's Master of Arts in Writing and Publishing program hands-on, practical experience in book publishing. The goal of Big Shoulders Books is to disseminate, free of charge, quality anthologies of writing by and about Chicagoans whose voices might not otherwise be shared. Each year, Big Shoulders Books hopes to make small but meaningful contributions to discussions of injustice and inequality in Chicago, as well as to celebrate the tremendous resilience and creativity found in all areas of the city.

The views and opinions expressed in this book do not necessarily reflect those of DePaul University or the College of Liberal Arts and Social Sciences, and should not be considered an endorsement by DePaul for any purpose.

ABOUT OUR FUNDERS

I Remember: Chicago Veterans of War was made possible by a grant from the William & Irene Beck Charitable Trust.

For those who are still fighting,
whether abroad or at home.

And in remembrance of Phil Hecker.

The Book's Format

I Remember: Chicago Veterans of War weaves together the memories of fifty veterans of World War II, Korea, Vietnam, Bosnia, Iraq, and Afghanistan. These vets were asked to submit any number of "I remember" statements— to recall the small and the large of their war experiences.

TEXT

The book lists veterans' memories one after the next with numbers instead of names in the margin to signal each new voice. Readers can, when and if they choose, check the Biography section in the back of the book to match a number and its associated memories with the name of a veteran and his or her background. Because of the near anonymity of the text, the book superficially appears to contain the memories of just one veteran—an attempt to emphasize the similarities of all wars. The system of numbering is also meant to be vaguely militaristic—a way of foregrounding the contrast between a soldier's number or unit and the unique human story of every war.

PHOTOS

Many of the veterans featured in the book contributed snapshots from their time in war; also, some of the veterans were photographed for the book. Like the memories, there are no names attached to the photographs. Each photo is listed by page number in the back of the book along with the name of its corresponding veteran.

Contents

Foreword

// **MANY YEARS AGO,** at a Powell's Bookstore in Lincoln Park, I stared at a title on a book spine: *A Country Made by War*. What country? I wondered stupidly. My ancestors had fought in the Revolutionary, Mexican, Seminole Indian and Civil Wars, besides chasing Apaches in Arizona Territory, and farther from home (in the British Army) in East Africa and Ottoman Iraq during World War I. My father had covered World War II's European theater as an on-the-spot correspondent; my great-great aunt, who'd lived in Paris through the Occupation, witnessed the arrival of the American Army. Me, I had humped central Vietnam's forested mountains as a grunt in the 101st Airborne Division. What country, indeed! I was still in a mode of forgetting war and hadn't yet begun my many returns, geographical and literary, to Vietnam.

So, yes, we're a country made by war. Our military forces have been busy ever since the Second Continental Congress created the Army, Navy and Marines in 1775. Since then about forty million citizen-soldiers have served the U.S. Today the American military—Army, Air Force, Navy, Marines and Coast Guard—is vast and varied, encompassing over 1,360,000 women and men on active duty and about 850,000 reservists. The fifty contributors to *I Remember* are a small cross-section yet reflect some of the variety and continuity of this history. They also reflect the universal experiences of soldiers going back in recorded history to the Trojan War.

The challenge of being a soldier, sailor or airman, in peacetime or at war, transforms people. Military service stands apart from the long, winding road of civilian life: high school, weddings, jobs, vacations, July 4th barbecues and endless summer afternoons at the ballpark. You're thrown together with other Americans whose unique backgrounds you couldn't imagine before—in one Chicagoan's recollection, "a barracks full of Texas and Oklahoma wranglers who chewed tobacco." You share stereotypical, yet vibrantly individual, experiences and rites of passage with them. Goodbye to Mom and Dad. Training. First weekend pass. Forming ties of duty and affection or even love, under trying circumstances, with strangers ("I remember the love," declares an Iraq vet). Shipping out—sometimes to faraway war zones and to combat or combat-support units. Coming home.

The return to the U.S. and civvy street is a mixed experience. Families are always happy to see their beloved returnees, but today's America—where ex-military personnel are a small minority—is not always a welcoming homeland. Beyond traditional veterans' groups, it's often hard for vets to get together, relax, share their life-transforming memories. And yet what memories this book's writers confide to the reader! The motif of beauty alone is an eye-opener. There are the "many shades of green," "desert roses," "Afghanis singing their morning prayers over the loudspeaker," and the question: "how could such a devastating and treacherous place hold such beauty?" One returnee from desert warfare writes, as if in counterpoint, about "how vivid the colors were when I returned home. That feeling of returning to beauty."

Given the fact that the U.S., the world's policeman for better or worse since 1945, has hundreds of bases and outposts overseas, encounters with foreign countries are another staple of veterans' recollections. Going abroad for the first time—and being young—is a fresh, striking experience that war magnifies. I remember riding under low monsoon clouds in the open back of a deuce-and-a-half truck through Huế, Vietnam's battered imperial city on Palm Sunday. Contributors to this book describe analogous places: Brussels, Venosa, Vienna, Guam, Inchon, Eniwetok Atoll, the A Shau Valley, Sarajevo, East Germany, the Korengal Valley, Helmand Province, Jalalabad, Fallujah, Guantanamo Bay, the vastness of the ocean or the night sky. What amazing places to be young or (like a fifty-year-old female Guardsman heading to Iraq) in the company of the young!

The transition from boy or girl to adult, speeded by the seriousness of military service, is an inevitable motif in these memoirs. It runs the gamut. One contributor recalls suppressing tears, after saying goodbye to his dad, by telling himself: "Act like a man." A woman recalls her glee:

"I was in ITALY, and my overprotective mother was an ocean away…I felt mischievously grown." Some marvel at being "fresh out of high school" and having to take on a shitload of responsibilities. Others embrace their unit ties: "for the first time ever I had brothers to look out for." Some learn to deal "with the pain of losing a brother in arms." Military service can be a primer in Mickey Mouse pettiness and the indoctrination of an over-simple worldview; as one contributor writes, "my young 21-year-old mind smelled bullshit from the beginning." It can be fatal, since young soldiers bear the burden of foreign policy decisions — and blunders — that our armed forces enact. Yet the military is also our nation's leading equal opportunity employer. Though some vets return home with scars and awful disabilities, others bring with them new skills, self-confidence and an enlarged sense of their American-ness.

Many contributors to this volume have gone to war. They have gone to World War II, "the good war" — Studs Terkel's ironic label. And they have gone to less obviously "good," controversial wars: Korea, Vietnam, Bosnia, Afghanistan and the Bush family's two Iraq wars. Though they were supported by troops honorably serving outside of war zones, they brought home different memories because war is unique and uniquely hard. But at least they did come home — unlike, say,

Milton Lee Olive III, an eighteen-year-old Medal of Honor winner whose memorial stands in the Streeterville park named after him.

Before war becomes a memory or a story, it is something that happens — a series of events right *here*, right *now* — which veterans remember and puzzle over afterwards. It differs from other experiences because its setting and its actions seem to belong to another, absurd realm where the Red Queen of battle really does cut off heads. Other venues and moments may be equally vivid, but war — the organized, deliberate use, when other strategies fail or are dismissed, of destruction and killing — challenges our prewar understanding of who we are and what the world is like. Our parents didn't teach us to be warriors.

The warrior's memories are a weight he or she carries for a long time. A thread in these recollections is survivor's guilt. One contributor captures the paradox of this syndrome: "the guilt I feel for my fallen friends is the only part of them I have left." This is a lesson of "The Lives of the Dead," the last story in Tim O'Brien's *The Things They Carried*. Other veterans of war find it hard to weave their experiences into the narrative of their civilian lives. *Post*-traumatic stress disorder is just that — it happens *after* the trauma and is reactivated by conscious and unconscious remembering.

But most vets overcome it, though they may have to do
so every day. A woman who served in Iraq comments:
"I remember we were all just kids. Now, I'm broken,
struggling to smile each day, but at least I do. Mourn. Heal.
Live." Remembering is always a process of interpreting and
reinterpreting. After our amazing or numbingly boring
or fulfilling or awful experiences—sometimes all these
adjectives apply—we veterans seek those experiences'
meaning. At odd moments or in college courses or therapy
or sustained conversations with other vets, we remember.
In a deeper, broader way than the military's tunnel-visioned
OR-LLs—Operational Reports-Lessons Learned—we
seek to understand. And, as time goes by, our understanding
changes in a way that the OR-LLs don't. The vivid, raw,
original experience of war—or of simply serving in the
military, a strange enough experience—becomes overlaid
with recollection. It is filtered by the individual lessons
that our older selves have learned from life. But that first,
vivid experience never goes away. We feel it in sudden,
unbidden memories. We feel it in dreams. We are veterans;
we remember.

JIM FAIRHALL

Introduction

// **ONE EVENING A FEW YEARS AGO,** I watched the incredible Chicago actor Tim Kane perform the one-man play *An Iliad*, a modern-day retelling of Homer's classic. The time is the present moment, the lone figure onstage is a storyteller called The Poet. He is fated to tell his story throughout history about the Trojan War, but also to convey the heroism and horror in all wars.

> Have you ever seen a front line? (*Shakes his head.*) Let's take—I want to show you what the bloody field looked like, what Hector walked back to just then, with all those other boys scattered across it. It's like, it's like—I have a picture here. (*He rifles through his suitcase.*) It's from another war but—oh, I can't—(*Can't find it.*)—well here. (*He holds up his hand instead, using it as a map.*)—you see, outside the trenches where there had been a particularly bad day—this was, oh, a hundred years ago but you get the picture—and uhhh the battlefield was just littered with bodies and when you look at it you think, "Oh, well these are a bunch of bodies," but they're not just bodies 'cuz this is—this is Jamie and this is Matthew and this is Brennan and this is Paul.[1]

Each war is unique, but all wars are the same. Grappling with the multitude of human casualties from an eternal war, The Poet repeatedly wills his memory to wake up. I was struck by the seeming helplessness of The Poet, but also stirred by the obvious importance of his telling, the necessity of remembering.

And what of the memories of the warriors themselves?
If we hear about war at all, it is rarely from soldiers. I'm a
poet, not a veteran, but as an observer I felt the need to hear
from veterans and I set out to ask Chicago vets to send me
memories of their wars. I knew only a few veterans. Less
than 1% of Americans have served in Iraq or Afghanistan[2]
… it seems America no longer goes to war, the military
does. I was invited to various VFW barbeques. I was eager
and asked as many veterans as I could if they might share
their memories. And then one vet pulled me aside and said
what is obvious now, but wasn't then: "The truth is most
vets don't want to remember."

So there was also the challenge of gaining trust. Every
veteran who submitted memories was accepted as a
contributor to the book. In other words, no veteran was
turned away or told their memories were not worthy
of being heard. I also thought that asking veterans to frame
their memories as a series of "I remember" statements
might make for an inviting refrain that would allow them
to write more freely. This idea comes from Joe Brainard's
marvelous (though decidedly non-militaristic) memoir,
I Remember, which is composed entirely of "I remember"
statements. A few of the veterans who contributed
to the book are writers, but most are not, and I sent all
potential contributors samples of Brainard's writing
in the hope that his honesty, imagery, specificity, and clarity
might serve as a model for their writing.

Throughout the book, each new veteran's set of "I remember"
statements is labeled by a number, not a name. This
anonymous structure is meant to foreground the similarities
of all wars. But in editing the memories, I tried to maintain
the unique voice, language, and syntax of each veteran. I
tried to honor what each veteran witnessed and experienced,
while also trying to select and edit memories with a poet's
eye and ear. In particular, I tried to highlight memories that
embody contradiction: to me, this is the strange core of
poetry and of war. The polarities of battle and boredom,
dying and singing, hunger and home, rage and love, are what
shape the complex memories of each veteran.

Indeed, it seems there's nothing that can't fit within a war.
For me, the variety of memories, the vastness and difference
of what veterans experience, was a surprise. But the real
shock was the terrible scale and surreal detail of what they
saw—a father blocking a convoy of Humvees holding
his dying son, Iraqi soldiers playing soccer with a severed
head, the first test and three-mile fireball of a hydrogen
bomb, and on and on.

But war isn't always its most dramatic self. As one veteran in the book, Elaine Little, says, "The truth is war is as much about waiting and preparation as actual engagement." Indeed, the veterans featured here held a variety of combat and non-combat roles: intel analyst, aircraft mechanic, truck driver, electrical engineer, pilot, radio operator, marksman, infantryman, paratrooper, hospital administrator, legal advisor, wireman, interrogator, journalist, linguist, psychological operations specialist, law enforcement officer, flight engineer, combat correspondent, computer operator, human resource specialist, finance specialist, operations officer, infantry platoon commander, recon platoon commander, information systems technician, combat engineer, military clerk typist, logistics officer, public information officer, boatwinmate, cryptographer, public health nurse, cargo specialist, stenographer, air traffic controller, telecommunications operator, and substance abuse counselor. And sometimes military labels for what human soldiers do sounds especially inhuman: for example, "PATRIOT Launching Station Enhanced Operator/Maintainer."

Please note that some of the roles given to soldiers end in the masculine, like "infantry*man*." Connie Meacham remembers, "Women were not allowed to use weapons or do the obstacle course in boot camp. There were no maternity uniforms. Sexual harassment was rampant and not talked about…I remember not many years later, they combined men's and women's barracks; women did combat training; and maternity uniforms were required of pregnant 'airmen.'" And while the historical exclusion and oppression of women in the military is clear, it's worth noting that some of the female veterans here also share important memories of meaningful male support and respect.

Also, I was surprised to find how very young so many of these men and women were when they enlisted, often entering the military at 17 or 18 years of age. Phil Hecker was a C-47 captain during D-Day dropping men and supplies over France: he logged 450 flight hours by the time he was 21. Only months after graduating from high school, Meosha Thomas found herself working in Intelligence, downloading top-secret messages after 9/11.

Yet despite the extraordinary experiences our soldiers face, rarely do veterans get to tell their stories. Like the war journalist and film maker Sebastian Junger, I believe if our country can't give veterans better health care or more money or fewer wars, then the least we can do is give them permission and opportunity to share their experiences:

The therapeutic power of storytelling, for example, could give combat veterans an emotional outlet and allow

civilians to demonstrate their personal involvement.
On Memorial Day or Veterans Day, in addition to
traditional parades, communities could make their city
or town hall available for vets to tell stories. Each could
get, say, 10 minutes to tell his or her experience at war.

Attendance could not be mandatory, but on that day
"I support the troops" would mean spending hours
listening to our vets. We would hear a lot of anger and
pain. We would also hear a lot of pride. Some of
what would be said would make you uncomfortable,
whether you are liberal or conservative, military or
nonmilitary, young or old. But there is no point in having
a conversation about war that is not completely honest.[3]

This anthology is what Junger might describe as Chicago's
city hall, and the honesty is offered by fifty veterans spanning
every modern war.

CHRIS GREEN

1. Lisa Peterson and Denis O'Hare, *An Iliad* (New York: Dramatists
Play Service, 2013).

2. James Fallows, "The Tragedy of The American Military,"
The Atlantic, January/February Issue, 2015.

3. Sebastian Junger, "U.S. Veterans Need to Share The Moral Burden
of War" (Opinion), *The Washington Post*, 24 May, 2013.

DONG HA · FDC BUNKER ·

I REMEMBER it when I wake up.
I remember the abrupt claps of gunfire and the rude whistling of rounds.
I remember an ovation of violence commencing—with these unrelenting sounds.
I remember clinging to each breath as my last, while I clutched the shaking ground.
I remember the hate inside my bullets as I shot back, scared and bound.
I remember the rhythm of battle: mnemonic like rhymes—as it surrounds.
I remember it in my dreams.

I remember it when I wake up.
I remember the abrupt claps of gunfire and the rude whistling of rounds.
I remember an ovation of violence commencing—with these unrelenting sounds.
I remember clinging to each breath as my last, while I clutched the shaking ground.
I remember the hate inside my bullets as I shot back, scared and bound.
I remember the rhythm of battle: mnemonic like rhymes—as it surrounds.
I remember it in my dreams.

2 I REMEMBER you Yazzie.

I remember the day you told me of your pregnant wife, and resounding fatherly pride.

I remember the time I saw you sitting on a cot with your weapon down.

I remember that February morning before the sun came up.

I remember when they said your name following KIA.

I remember the lieutenant crying when he heard the news.

I remember you Yazzie.

I remember when you waved goodbye.

3 I REMEMBER . . . shots.

I remember the muffled 'pock, pock' of M-14s, other units moving out to our left through sand and pines.

I remember Fort Polk, autumn 1968. Night training, ITT. Parachute flares descending, an ambient glow penetrating the forest canopy.

I remember . . . shots.

I remember cholera, an epidemic on the land. We medics at the base camp
gate wielded pneumatic vaccine guns while the MPs wielded M-16s for
crowd control. Outside the wire, lines of wary rice farmers, waiting women in
sarongs, old Mamasans, infants swaddled in their arms.

I remember . . . shots.

I remember R&R in Bangkok, a day of brilliant sun, scents and singing bells on the
canals and floating markets, silks, melons, bowls of beaten silver, sensual hibiscus.

I remember a headline on the cover of the English language Bangkok Post
at my hotel—"U.S. Army shoots down students on Ohio campus!"

I remember . . . shots.

I remember jiggers of sloe gin and draughts of Singha, one after another,
a sheaf of red 500 baht bills strewn between me and the attentive bartender
(the King of Thailand in full dress uniform looks out from the crisp currency).

I remember a slender and too young woman in heels and silken sheath
approached and brushed her taut hip against my thigh.

I remember Hemingway's Frederick Henry.

I remember I pushed through the dark door of teak and heavy glass, and walked
back to the hotel in the rain.

4   I REMEMBER I was sleeping on the ground between two rocks in a valley.

I remember, covered in filth from the day, I was scared for my life.

I remember I felt no matter what, I was not going to make it home.

I remember six separate air insertions.

I remember a dark valley with no moon.

I remember men wielding Kalashnikovs looking to kill our roving patrol.

I remember sheer blackness, the faint glow of our cat eyes.

I remember hours asking myself why. Why was I here? Why would I put my family through this?

I remember I was a paratrooper and the foremost tip of our great country's spear.

I remember the War on Terror.

I remember no one ever told me that God looks on paratroopers with great favor.

I remember I sat up in that dirt—in that valley—where rangers and other special operators had just lost their lives.

I remember I sat there and wondered who am I, and why did I deserve not to die?

I remember after three tours of duty, I was never killed by an IED. I was not shot by a sniper. I was never stabbed. I was not burned alive. I never lost an eye or a limb.

I remember those that were hurt or died while we were making right by our country.

I remember a dedicated paratrooper. I remember him in the back of his vehicle in Iraq and blown so far away by a roadside bomb that no one could find him for hours.

I remember his smile and demeanor and I wonder why. I could go on, but only to prove that my mind is slipping and my brain is full of holes.

5   I REMEMBER when I was the dismount team leader on our typical IED route
clearance up the Korengal Valley. My job was to dismount the vehicle and
investigate possible IEDs on foot with a small team. It was not always IEDs
that we got out for.

I remember in this specific situation, it was a father holding his son in his arms
refusing to move out of our path. Bird (who was later killed on a second
deployment to Afghanistan) and I found the boy barely holding onto his life.

I remember we ended up moving to the rear of the convoy to talk to the
commander with the man and his son, but by the time we made the two-minute
walk, the life of the boy escaped him. I will never forget that boy's brown eyes.

6 I REMEMBER feeling infinite at night.

I remember being on a cruiser in the middle of the Pacific Ocean with no lights or sounds and stars stretched from horizon to horizon.

I remember the feeling watching the fathometer approaching zero.

I remember the instant at which 10,000 tons of steel would smash into the ocean bottom at 30 plus knots. 64 ft., 41 ft., 25 ft., 17 ft. We continued the swing at full speed, hard rudder.

I remember I looked at my conning officer, a green ensign who started to shake—10 ft., 6 ft., 3 ft.

I remember the cruiser continued its swing, the rudder thrown all the way over.

I remember no lights and hundreds of contacts on the radar.

I remember it was a matter of faith and vectors.

7 I REMEMBER a cold, crisp wind cut through my sleeping bag as I lay in the dirt dreading what was to come. I had been on many missions before, but this one felt different. Moreno was already awake packing up his gear. I could hear Hay's watch alarm beeping from the distance. Our COP, or combat outpost, was not very big, small enough where I could throw a football from all corners. I followed the sound right to Hays; he was cuddled up in a ball behind the trailer full of dried foods. He was notorious for eating the last of our rations.

I remember it was pitch black and we were on our way, each one of us in our full kit layered with armor, ammo, and a 60-pound rucksack with supplies and more ammo.

I remember we had a six-mile journey ahead of us, two villages, three peaks, and a mountain, before digging into our positions where we would lie motionless for the next three days.

I remember smelling a village fire. I could hear dogs howling in the distance. We crossed a 100-foot river. It deepened with every step I took, felt as if I was walking in ice.

I remember we were forced to skirt the outside of the village. The walls made of mud, and their doors made of sheets.

I remember we were ants on a mission, one behind the other evenly spaced as we tracked across the desert.

I remember hearing in the distance the Afghanis singing their morning prayers over the loudspeaker.

I remember welcoming the warmth of the rising sun as it enveloped us.

I remember thinking, how could such a devastating and treacherous place hold such beauty?

I remember the squad was silent. We scanned our sectors.

8 I REMEMBER becoming a Marine Sharpshooter: Rifle Range, Camp Pendleton 1966—

Dawn

Windage flags

The low fog lifting.

Chilly ocean air warming
gradually.

Target numbers downrange becoming visible through the gray morning mist.

The smell of cordite—almost like incense—

      following the first round of firing from the 200 yard

         off-hand position line.

The crunchy, black cinder under our boots.

The sharp "tang" as the empty brass cartridge springs out the ejector of my M-14
and twirls past my ear to "plink" against other empty cartridges on the ground behind
me. The humid smell in the damp leather of my shooting glove late in the afternoon.

"Ready on the right? Ready on the left? Ready on the firing line. Watch downrange
shooters," echoing over the rifle range.

The soft moaning ambulance siren receding as they take Strickhorn away.

BRASS

Breathe
Relax
Aim
Slack
Squeeze
        your trigger

The tacky feel of stickum on the shoulder of my shooting jacket
keeping the metal butt plate from slipping even a millimeter

down.

9 I REMEMBER the cultural shock of jumping, in 1943, from the freshman class of the University of Chicago, where I studied The Great Books under Hutchins and didn't know much else at 19, and suddenly being plunged into the Mule Pack, a branch of the field artillery arm that specialized in loading howitzers on the backs of mules, driving them up mountains and shooting the guns down at enemies below. I found myself in a barracks full of Texas and Oklahoma wranglers who chewed tobacco, spoke a strange version of English and liked to gamble and drink and chase. I didn't know anything about any of these things, but I learned.

I remember a very cold very early Christmas morning in France, jouncing around in the back of an Army truck, looking through bleary eyes at the highway reeling away from me and the dock where we had just disembarked, now and then a shot-up German armored vehicle perched on the high roadside banks slipping by and our mammoth howitzer lunging and jerking just behind.

I remember the hollow feeling in my stomach: hunger or fear?

I remember it didn't go away after we had messed with the rest of our battalion that evening at an abandoned hangar in Rennes. Just an acre of concrete covered by a corrugated steel roof that had been punctured by shrapnel and that didn't give much shelter from a slow, cold night rain. We spread our blankets in the driest place we could find and tried to sleep. It was hard, with the occasional bang of a truck door and the whoops of a drunk GI on the far side. We were going into combat the next day, I was sure. I sorted through my feelings. Yeah, it was fear, and I didn't like it.

I remember, two months later, after we had done some shooting and received some incoming, getting a pass for four days in London. I was in one of those London cabs with a lawn mower engine and a back end so roomy I could stand up—all of the scrawny six feet two inches of me. But I didn't because I was afraid of irritating my fellow passengers who had had to share the cab with me, a bad match. They were tall, formally dressed elderly aristocrats, headed for an embassy party I guessed. They murmured to each other with an accent I recognized only from the movies. He wore a pince-nez! I was uncomfortable— I wanted to speak to them, but was pretty sure they didn't want to speak to me.

I remember a few months after the war's end, the formerly awesome St. Stephens Cathedral in Vienna, lying in an awkward sprawl across the boulevard, knocked down by the Russian artillery; and how impossibly cold the nights were. There were gaunt Austrians with their faces pressed against the windows of the cafes where we occupying Americans were fed—on tables with white linen tablecloths, cut glass decanters and silver flatware, with string quartets playing Mozart, the best food I've ever tasted. In the mornings, trucks dumped potatoes on the sidewalk and workers with scoops shoveled them down chutes.

I remember a long line of GIs snaking across a parking lot in Marseilles, ending at a tractor trailer inside of which two whores were servicing them, one man every fifteen minutes.

I remember the feelings, after my discharge after three years of service meeting my mother and brothers at the copper doors of the Kansas City train station with a mixture of anticipation and a little fear, not unlike what I felt at that hangar in Rennes.

10 I REMEMBER when I arrived in Germany—the Berlin Wall still intact and the Soviet Union still a super power.

I remember Central Europe as clean and Eastern Europe as gray with grime covering centuries old structures from the exhaust of factories and Trabants—the pastel colored cars of East Germany.

I remember the traffic on the autobahn grid-locked and hundreds of thousands of protesters swarmed everywhere.

I remember the world had seemed to stop to protest the Persian Gulf War.

I remember signs, "Kein krieg fur ol," hanging from windows of businesses and apartment buildings and car windows.

I remember German police in full riot gear standing atop large green water trucks with long powerful hoses.

I remember being surrounded by color, noise, and opposition. The protesters so numerous, feeling as if we were flowing down a river.

I remember praying hard. Our vehicle like a boat in a body of water.

11 I REMEMBER I was going from Seoul, Korea to join my ship in Inchon Harbor. I was riding in an open truck in my sailor's dress blues and white hat.

I remember on the truck were a number of Marines who had been wounded and were returning to the front.

I remember one of them suggested I remove my white hat. There were snipers in the area.

I remember the first night out we stopped in a burned-out house.

I remember one of the Marines gave me half of his mess kit.

I remember that night, my two beautiful white blankets issued to all sailors, and the burned-out dirty floor.

I remember a Marine to my rescue, again. He gave me half of his shelter to put under my blankets.

[12] I REMEMBER Marine Corps history, customs, and traditions; close order drill; fire team and squad tactics; inspections: personal, junk on the bunk, rifle.

I remember a lot of platoon circles in-between and in the evenings.

I remember we took showers with our utilities on and with our rifles.

I remember my parents took the train from Chicago to Quantico for the commissioning.

I remember my first duty as Officer-of-the-Day was on Christmas Eve. A dozen Marines asked if they could use a six-by and go caroling main side. Why not! When we got back, the SMF CO was waiting. He chewed me out then gave me a bottle of scotch to share with my crew.

13 I REMEMBER very clearly being shot at by shore battery. During return fire for hours, the TEC was finally hit by a 105mm. We turned around and went after the gun mount, finally taking it out once and for all. We were hit a second time just below the waterline in the engine room—put a big dimple in the hull. We found the damage: the shell should have taken out the fuel line to the boiler. If that shell weren't a dud, I would probably not be writing this.

14 I REMEMBER thinking, "He's dead. He's fucking dead." Only to have him grab my arm and scream, "Sgt. Z don't let me die!"

I remember waking to the blast as another of our guys was hit by an IED no farther than 200 meters outside of our COP.

I remember talking to Grata about scanning our sector. The next thing I know I wake up on top of Grata who is screaming about his ears ringing. I can see SSG. Chavez screams at us, but I can't make out the words.

I remember Villareal trying to break open a piñata, only to fall on his ass.

I remember our slogan, "It's just another day in the DAB."

I remember, every year I remember.

I remember waking up day after day, thinking it was only a matter of time before I was hit again. The fucked up part was that we were all okay with it. It wasn't a question of am I gonna get hit? It was merely, is it gonna be my left leg that gets blown off or my right one?

15 I REMEMBER my first operation was humping the boonies. Probably 100 degrees, through jungle, up and down what I called mountains. Squad leader Terry Hardig took my heavy pack and gave me his very light one. First lesson in camaraderie.

I remember later Terry stepped on a land mine and was KIA.

I remember being ambushed. Two of my best friends were killed when a rocket landed in the middle of our group. Al had his face blown off, and Ed had wounds all over his body. I was no more than three feet away and yet I am still here today.

16 I REMEMBER praying only once in Vietnam…I prayed for my sanity.

I remember B-52 bombers at night lighting up the sky for miles and the ground shaking.

I remember using a big rock as a pillow.

I remember during Tet telling my guys, "Lock and load…they're coming."

17 I REMEMBER the smell of rotting flesh and cordite.

I remember the mornings were beautiful with the sound of the birds waking up.

[18] I REMEMBER we would fly out over the North Atlantic to a specific location and then fly in a small circle for hours on end sending a Morse code message to pilots that basically said, "We are here. Fly toward us."

I remember the sad part, of course, was that the president died and a new era started.

I remember during that year I flew thousands of miles and saw thousands of square miles of snow and water.

I remember the last flight of Shadow 78.

I remember while training in Ohio, I drove to Omaha and proposed to my girlfriend, Barbara. The possibility that I might not survive was left unspoken.

I remember combat missions five nights in a row.

I remember all flights were flown between sunset and sunrise.

I remember this flight would have been around my 60th combat mission.

I remember our call sign word, which would be "Shadow 78" for that night's flight.

I remember we were strapped in on the gun deck. I was just forward of #1 gun.

I remember they declared an emergency. There was "dead air."

I remember the left engine was feathered.

I remember the flare launcher, which weighed about 2500 lbs.

I remember I could feel myself burning. I think Fage and Van were being burned too.

I remember the right wall opened up and the engine carried both of them out of the plane.

I remember I didn't want to remember what I had seen.

I remember I raced away from the plane. I knew my hands were burning and I think my head was too.

I remember I was air-evacuated to the burn ward at Camp Zama in Japan.

I remember two times a day I was taken for treatment in the bath. I was lowered into a warm whirlpool bath and as the water softened the bandages and skin, nurses debrided (picked off) the bandages and dead skin.

I remember going to the Vietnam Memorial Wall in Washington, D.C. for the first time. I stood in front of Panel 11W, looking at lines 62 through 66.

19 I REMEMBER going home from basic via bus, rather than Trans Texas Airline, which was called Try Try Again.

I remember my Steno 12 Class at Ft. Ben Harrison in Indianapolis. It lasted four months. I took Gregg shorthand at 120 words per minute.

I remember flying from Chicago, Illinois to Ft. Dix, New Jersey and then back across the country to California, Hawaii, Guam, and then Vietnam.

I remember being assigned to work for BG Jack MacFarlane as his stenographer.

I remember pictures when I got an award or promotion—my boss was 6 ft. 7, and I was 5 ft. 4.

I remember my trip home from Nam. Cam Rahn Bay to Japan, to Seattle, to Chicago O'Hare.

I remember the welcome by my parents who met me at the airport. I also remember a sign they made that said *Welcome Home* in front of our house on Narragansett.

20 I REMEMBER how vivid the colors were when I returned home. That feeling of returning to beauty.

I remember a mission out of Afghanistan where we transported a fallen soldier back home. He had died in a firefight that morning.

I remember his close friend who had fought alongside him and who traveled with his remains all the way back home. Since he would be presenting the casket to the fallen soldier's family, his friends tried to make him as presentable as possible. They gave him a sport coat that was much too large, a white collared shirt that was much too small, and a pair of khaki pants. What stood out the most though was the dried blood that he had not been able to wash off in his haste. You could see where he tried to wash his face, but dried blood remained around his hairline and beard.

I remember for the entire seven-hour flight, he did not move from his seat next to his friend's casket. Not once to use the bathroom. Not once to get a drink of water. Not once to get something to eat.

21   I REMEMBER the unbearable cold embedded into my bones.

I remember how hungry I was, my food gritty with sand but still it tasted so good.

I remember the smell of diesel fluid.

I remember waking up with the outdoors, sleeping under the stars, how bright the night sky was and how many stars.

I remember these moments of peace in my long day and days ahead.

I remember how proud I was to wear my uniform, the traditions behind it I had earned.

I remember coming home.

I remember the frustrations of long lines and not understanding things, feeling lost in a big city.

I remember my family.

22 I REMEMBER seeing my brother Bernie's face in a tent in Venosa, Italy during World War II.

I remember he considered me a kid. I looked up to him as my oldest brother. When he got married I was twelve years old. Bernie went into the infantry and he was at the Battle of Anzio where he was injured. As a 114 lb. 18-year-old from Chicago, I went to Italy with the Fifteenth Air Force as a flight engineer on a B24. As a clerk in Naples, Bernie saw the shipping orders of my arrival into Naples.

I remember one evening I and the other six guys in my tent were on our cots in sleeping bags to keep warm. Our conversation was interrupted as the tent door opened. In walked my brother Bernie. He was hunched over from the long, cold journey but he had a huge smile on his face. I was so excited I jumped out of my sleeping bag without unzipping it. I had not seen him in two years. I couldn't believe my big brother hitchhiked across Italy, partly in the dark and mud, to see me. Bernie wrote a ten page letter home about this trip. He said, "I can't describe the emotion of seeing Gil after being apart two years. I can't get over my kid brother, his position as flight engineer and crew chief."

I remember after the war we became equals.

I remember being on a flight mission to a shipping yard in Vienna. The shrapnel from the anti-aircraft guns was very intense. The sky was black with flak. I could not imagine surviving this onslaught without getting hit. I remember thinking about how if I had to bail out, what I should do with my dog tags.

They were stamped with the letter H for Hebrew. If I took them off, and survived the jump, I might get captured then killed as a spy. If I left them on, I might get killed as a Jew. As it turned out, although we did get pieces of shrapnel through the plane, it was not serious. I never did decide if I should leave the dog tags on or take them off.

23 I REMEMBER my first weekend pass, drunk on my bunk thinking about the Chicago Cubs opening day.

I remember that cold Missouri night and another Chicago GI. We came up with a brilliant idea. We were going to hitchhike back to Chicago.

I remember a happy-go-lucky guy saying he was on his way to New York. He could drop us in Chicago if we would do the driving.

I remember the feelings of freedom.

I remember the dark sides of the highway, like an edge into the void.

I remember seeing Interstate 57 and knew it wouldn't be long.

24 I REMEMBER seeing a little girl on a big white water buffalo.

I remember I ran toward her to take a picture (I had no weapon, only a camera), but she saw my face, my green fatigues and was terrified.

I remember waking up in the morning and smelling burning feces. The thick black clouds choked and gagged us despite the winds or the calm.

I remember going to shows the Army would set up once a month or so, looking up at the stars and thinking how far I was from home.

I remember getting home after 11 months and 17 days and playing the first song that came on the radio: "Ain't No Mountain High Enough" by Diana Ross and the Supremes.

25 I REMEMBER Basic Training in Orlando, Florida: the very early morning cool, misty air, and the smell that was so different than Chicago—like country, like grass. Then the mist would lift and the sun would begin to get hot, and then I knew, really knew, I was someplace other than home.

26 I REMEMBER Master Sergeant, E-8, and Rodgers. He was my NCO on my first tour to Vietnam. Now this ain't no BS. Since I had gone through the Special Warfare School with the Special Forces at Fort Bragg, NC, I was assigned to a Military Advisory Command, Vietnam (MACV) unit in Nha Trang.

I remember our battalion was responsible for the security of the railroad trains that ran over 200 miles of track in the center of Vietnam. 200 miles, every day.

I remember, during my year, there was only one attack on a train. A mine was set off under one of the cars that killed a teenager selling ice cream.

I remember there was once an explosion of a different sort. It sounded like a large satchel charge with a lot of C4. After that, it was small arms fire all over the place. It was Tet of '68 and we immediately headed for our Vietnamese battalion behind the railway station.

I remember bodies were lying all along the route and I had my M2 carbine ready. (All of our weapons were WWII. There must have been an immense stockpile of leftover equipment left behind in the Philippines. Even our jeeps and C-rations were WWII.)

I remember I heard a number of "whooshes" pass by. I asked Sergeant Rodgers about that sound. Slow, even, calm, with little emotion, he said, "They were bullets passing by. If you don't hear them, you're dead." "Why," I asked, "did we stand in an open courtyard?" He explained it was a remnant of the French showing no fear.

27 I REMEMBER this day in particular I was shamming (skipping out on work) with my squad at Patrick Henry Mall in Ft. Eustis, Virginia. Our squad leader was cool and let us change out of our uniforms and put on civilian clothes. We were at the movies in the middle of the day watching *Malibu's Most Wanted* starring Jamie Kennedy.

I remember our squad leader got a call that we had to report to formation ASAP and that the rear detachment came down on orders to deploy to Iraq and be with the rest of our platoon.

I remember many of us were incredibly young. We were fresh out of high school.

I remember we were scheduled to leave in 72 hours. I called my mom back home in Chicago and told her I couldn't do it and that I am *not* going to go! She told me to calm down and say a prayer.

I remember all the time leading up to departure time, I refused to pack. I sat in my (newly decorated) room at the barracks and maintained that I was *not* going. I didn't get anything ready. Was I really about to go AWOL? I didn't know.

I remember in the last possible moments I had left, I started flinging stuff everywhere. Packing my rucksack and my duffle bag. I had 24 bottles of Aquafina water on the floor by my bed. I was going to Iraq. I thought there would be no water, so I packed them *all* in my duffle bag!

I remember my bag was so heavy—I was dragging it. If I was going to Iraq, this water was going with me.

I remember at 0400 hours the morning of departure we boarded a bus headed toward the air base where the aircraft was waiting to take us over.

I remember I was 18 years old. That was the absolute last time in my life I ever felt fear.

28 I REMEMBER my father drove me to Glenview Naval Air Station to catch a flight to boot camp. But what I remember most was my father's eyes watering as I got out of the car. My father, who never showed emotion, was trying to control himself. I remember taking ten, maybe twenty steps away from the car and totally losing it. I began to cry hard and turned to run after my father as he drove away. I did not catch him. I stopped and thought to myself, *My God, you're nineteen. Get a hold of yourself. Act like a man.*

29 I REMEMBER I was a hot teenager all of 18, new to the military. I was in ITALY, and my overprotective mother was an ocean away and scared to fly. For the first time I felt mischievously grown.

I remember the day was September 11, 2001. I was on duty—my job to download the top-secret message traffic and give it to the squadron duty officer (SDO).

I remember everyone in the office was silent, fixated on the TV. I asked, "What movie are you all watching?"

I remember the SDO turned to me and said, "It's not a movie. It's real. We are going to war."

I remember the word war rolled off his tongue, the sirens and alarms went off, the whole world seemed to be screaming at the same time.

I remember I was the only person at the command who worked in Intelligence that day. I downloaded more top-secret messages, which were coming in like waves, for three days straight (Al-Qaeda's next possible targets).

I remember the military changed forever, the U.S. changed forever, the world changed forever . . . and just months before, I was in high school. Now I was key personnel in a war.

30 I REMEMBER how intense the heat and sun were.

I remember and still talk to all my brothers and sisters that I met because of that war.

I remember how good it was to have steady income.

I remember how I never wanted to miss a day of work because I was needed.

31 I REMEMBER meeting my Marines for the very first time during our deployment flights to the front lines of eastern Afghanistan.

I remember the intense heat and heavy battle-rattle while patrolling arduous desert plains.

I remember temperatures exceeding 120 degrees Fahrenheit and freezing winter nights.

I remember helicopter insertions and sniper missions in the mountain tree lines of the Korangal Valley.

I remember mortar and rocket attacks in the middle of the night.

I remember trained calmness looking for IEDs and roadside bombs.

I remember visiting small villages comprised only of dirt compounds and walls, where generations of families and tribes never ventured outside their immediate surroundings.

I remember enjoying watermelon at a forward operating base on July 4th, and from time to time the local footbread and goat meat as a welcomed break from warm water and MREs.

I remember my parents waiting for me when I got off the bus at 3rd Battalion 6th Marines Headquarters, Camp Lejeune, North Carolina.

I remember deploying back to combat operations in the Middle East.

I remember the energy and alertness of my Marines as we moved city block by city block — with tanks, military dogs, EOD, journalists, and linguists attached.

I remember not sleeping, thinking only of the well-being of my Marines.

I remember the high metallic density during sustained roof top firefights with the enemy in urban areas of Iraq.

I remember daily vigilance, never knowing where the enemy may be hiding.

I remember the dedicated interpreters who truly revered the Coalition Forces and wanted to see Iraq become a free country.

I remember rare satellite phone calls back home and my mom sending me anything that I asked for and more.

I remember my parents waiting for me when I got off the bus at 3rd Battalion 6th Marines Headquarters, Camp Lejeune, North Carolina.

32 I REMEMBER Guantanamo Bay. I sat about 20 feet away from KSM. Little fellow. He had a huge orange beard. The press was all in attendance. He made a paper airplane and tossed it into the air. It was eerie—court was silent. We pulled internal security for the trials. We tried the Cole bomber too. The defense was a bunch of smoke and mirrors.

I remember the tour was hot and long. My parents picked me up at O'Hare. Never have I appreciated a Chicago wind chill so much. The aroma of burnt fuel was intoxicating mixed with a cold sharp gust of air.

33 I REMEMBER with the way things were in the world, my generation grew up with the specter of nuclear war.

I remember that specter, from my point of view, was never more clear while on a prime target base. I made a promise to myself that if that day came, and we launched missiles, I would race home to my quarters in base housing. I wanted to be with my wife, the woman I love, so that the two of us could face the "fireball" together.

I remember the height of my Air Force career came while assigned to headquarters, SAC (Strategic Air Command) JSTPS (Joint Strategic Targeting and Planning Staff).

I remember the SAC Underground, a multi-level facility where I had to descend five flights of stairs.

I remember the few enlisted, like me, were "runners." We would go to the computer section in the main building to retrieve computer listings and drop off computer runs. I had a desk. It was about three foot square. There was a window frame with a fluorescent light inside to make it look like there was daylight coming through and of course a painting of a grass field and a bird.

I remember I worked on a very early type of the internet. They called it SACCOS (Don't ask. I don't remember.)

I remember the SAC side of JSTPS where the planners worked on their part of the SIOP, Single Integrated Operating Plan, a.k.a., the war plan. The planners orchestrated all nuclear weapons delivery, whether they were from land base missile, submarines, or dropped from aircraft. Every device had a target.

I remember the day I was asked to "flip" at the next briefing. Briefing charts and graphics were on transparent plastic sheets. These sheets would be placed on an overhead projector. I would flip the charts/plastic sheets in the inside room. The briefer used a clicker to signal me to flip the next chart. The classification of this briefing was very high. The audience was newly assigned commanders and crew members. I flipped and I listened. All of the new words that were being used became much more clear. I understood the mission of SAC and their motto, "Peace Is Our Profession." To this day, when asked what I did in the Air Force, I can say, "I participated in the formulation of thermonuclear war."

34 I REMEMBER Sarajevo. The snipers were gone. But there were still casualties. A local was hit and killed by falling bricks from a decaying building.

I remember there were little red crosses affixed to a rope that kept you from walking too close.

I remember the Bosnians did not like us on the whole. We were too late. Where were we when the markets were bombed and people picked off?

I remember my first and last Special Forces mission in Afghanistan. We traveled in a convoy from Bagram to Jalalabad. There were snow-capped mountains and ice-strewn streams.

I remember being excited to leave Bagram where I worked as an interrogator at the detention facility. I was now sent to search Afghan women crossing the border from Pakistan.

I remember being pleasantly surprised by the Special Forces' lack of bravado.

I remember that I never once felt like an interloper or an impediment— I felt respect.

I remember I experienced the truth that war is as much about waiting and preparation as actual engagement.

35 I REMEMBER being stationed in Norfolk, Virginia in 1943. I was part of a group called LION Six (Landing Infantry of the Navy). On June 4, 1944, two days before D-Day, Lion Six boarded two ships and sailed under the Golden Gate Bridge.

I remember our ship the Welterveden.

I remember landing on Guam on the second day of the invasion. I was part of a group of 100 men who called themselves the Fighting 100. Once the island was secured, Guam became a B-29 base where planes could take off for attacks on Japan.

36 I REMEMBER, as a 50-year-old guardsman deploying to Iraq, waiting for hours for a plane to Kuwait. I wore 45 pounds of gear: my Kevlar helmet, TA 50 (a belt with a gas mask, pistol, 2 canteens and ammo pouches, first aid, etc.), body armor, and one heavy backpack slung over my shoulder.

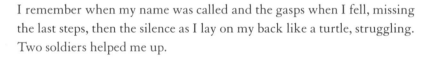

I remember when my name was called and the gasps when I fell, missing the last steps, then the silence as I lay on my back like a turtle, struggling. Two soldiers helped me up.

I remember there were at least 120 soldiers who saw my fall. For the many hours on the flight, it felt like each of the 120 asked me if I was alright.

37 I REMEMBER the hot, dry air.

I remember my life was about to change forever.

I remember the distance growing louder.

I remember the explosion.

I remember the sirens and alarms. I was not at home . . . I was in Afghanistan.

I remember my first indirect fire.

38 I REMEMBER when women were not allowed to use weapons or do the obstacle course in boot camp. There were no maternity uniforms. Sexual harassment was rampant and not talked about.

23 MEACHAM W157
CONSTANCE L.

I remember when I was arrested on Barksdale Air Force Base (1975) in Shreveport, Louisiana by an MP for sitting in a room in the men's barracks with the door open reviewing vocabulary words with a friend for an English test. My commander came to get me out and told me, "Please don't even think about this again." Go CO!

I remember not many years later, they combined men's and women's barracks; women did combat training; and maternity uniforms were required of pregnant "airmen."

39 I REMEMBER deplaning outside of Saigon, South Vietnam. I saw a pole with signs pointing all over the world—Los Angeles 3000 miles, New York 4800, etc. I was scared to death. I had volunteered for the draft. My new wife was pregnant. And I was headed into a war.

40 I REMEMBER it like a punch to the gut. Mat had been killed in combat.

I remember the war in Afghanistan never felt real until that moment.

I remember Mat as more than one heroic act.

I remember him as the man you looked to in moments of confusion.

41 I REMEMBER the smell when a C-130 came in.

I remember when the back ramp was lowered, and the loadmaster was wearing his gas mask—then we knew, it was remains in a body bag.

I remember coffins covered with the U.S. flag we sent back home from Vietnam.

I remember being unable to go on a training mission with 18 unit members. I asked someone else to replace me. The plane bringing them home crashed, killing everyone.

42 I REMEMBER the terror of the air war over Kosovo.

I remember the fear of supersonic booms!

I remember the medical missions.

I remember the distances Bosnian nurses traveled across mountains.

I remember seeing the surroundings (museums and parks) used as burial grounds.

43 I REMEMBER hearing the telltale pop of the departing rocket, faintly audible far off in the distance. *Shit, hear it comes*, I thought. Immediately, everyone within earshot of one another was on the same frequency, and for a frozen instant, no one moved. Then someone cried out loud and clear: "Incoming!" The dreaded word resonated over the hilltop. Seconds later the warning was repeated a little way off: "Incoming!"—and the panic-inducing bulletin spread like wildfire. I didn't waste a step. I seized my rifle and helmet and made a dash for the nearest foxhole. To be above ground when a round impacts is like being suddenly naked in a crowd.

This was LZ Cunningham, a hilltop astride the A Shau Valley. Every day about the same time—usually once in the morning, afternoon, then late at night—they hit us with rocket barrages. This long-range ordnance is usually harmless as long as it misses by a large margin; direct hits and close calls were another matter. As the weather turned we knew it was only a matter of time before they'd try to overrun us. Once socked in and without resupply, we'd be vulnerable. The choppers would not fly in the fog; we'd run low on ammo and C-rats.

I remember the grunts were dug in on the perimeter, protected by concertina wire and Claymore mines. They were our first line of defense against Charlie. Farther up, 50-caliber machine gunners bolstered our defenses. The 105's sat atop the hill to fire in support of our grunts humping it in the jungle—or down on the line if our situation turned dire. And then, the thick heavy clouds settled in, draped over us like a huge, suffocating flying carpet. Just to breathe in the heavy air was an effort.

44 I REMEMBER loud engulfing noise: painful, inescapable noise. As a combat arms officer, noise was the job: the screech and wail of a tank's metal parts grinding and the piercing high-pitched sound of a helicopter's turbines. All that was base-line noise. Combine that with the shattering, diaphragm thumping concussions of weapons and you have a recipe that deadens the ability to think. Repetitive concussions of heavy machine gun fire, sharp crackles of rifle fire, detonations of mortar rounds, or mines exploding. Tank main gun cannons could beat the breath from your chest with their shockwaves. But you must manage the violence around you, must think and communicate in the midst of it. The radio light comes on in your vehicle and you must connect: Is it the artillery adjusting your fire? The Air Force sending jets? One of your platoons in close contact with the enemy? The medivac helicopter needs a smoke grenade popped to find your LZ? The task is much like being inside a trash can full of fire crackers being rolled down the world's longest staircase. But the radio call light still glows and you must try to answer.

I remember colors. The fresh green of newly issued jungle fatigues, so new they hadn't been washed yet. Then seeing the faded green, almost light gray, of an officer's uniform who is awaiting his flight back to the states. He shared the barracks, but not the same reality. He didn't want to talk in case, somehow, that would delay his departure back to "the world." The jungle could be many shades of green. Not like the old Tarzan movies, but a forest of varying hues. The soil could be fertile black in many low-country rice paddies. The ground elsewhere could be an umber or sienna rust, dust or mud, depending upon the season. Then there was the brown of areas sprayed with Agent Orange. And the black of the dead trees in the same regions poking skyward as if after a forest fire. Not burned, but killed all the same. And those of us who operated in the area carried that poison back with us in our body's cells to kill us later. And the sky could be blue, supporting puffy clouds and providing backdrop for palm trees, looking like a poster for one of those 1930's airline Clipper travel jaunts. Or it could be filled with dark, roiling gray storm clouds shedding their rain day in and day out for months. Clouds that blocked the sun.

45 I REMEMBER we were shipped to Eniwetok Atoll 2500 miles southwest of Hawaii. I was part of a group of 20 cryptographers in the Signal unit. We were to handle the communications for Operation Ivy, which consisted of two tests: Mike, a hydrogen device, which was being tested for the first time, and King, an atomic bomb. A hydrogen bomb is made of an atomic bomb and, in this case, frozen liquid hydrogen. The atomic bomb is the trigger. We evacuated the islands and boarded the U.S.S. Estes.

I remember the morning of Mike (8 AM, November 1, 1952). We were moored about 30 miles from Elugelab, the test-site island. We were issued 1/2 inch thick smoky goggles for viewing the explosion. If you didn't have them, you had to turn your back to the direction of the explosion.

I remember standing by the rail of the Estes waiting for who knew what. The ten second countdown ended and in a nanosecond there on the horizon was the brightest half sun I had ever seen, even through the goggles.

I remember the heat, shock, and the low rumble of the explosion. The fireball quickly lost its glow and from it rose a radioactive debris-laden pillar that reached over 100,000 feet, mushroomed out, and stayed there until we came back on deck about 5 PM. The fireball was three miles across. The explosive force was equivalent to 10.4 million tons of TNT. Our cryptography then began, enciphering top-secret messages as they piled up by the dozens.

I remember we returned to Parry and prepared for King, an airdrop that exploded about 8 miles from us over Runit Island. It had an explosive force

January 31, 1950

My dear Mr. Lilienthal:

　　After consideration of the report by the Special Committee of the National Security Council consisting of the Secretary of State, the Secretary of Defense, and the Chairman of the Atomic Energy Commission, designated by me to advise me on this problem, I hereby direct the Atomic Energy Commission to proceed to determine the technical feasibility of a thermonuclear weapon, the scale and rate of effort to be determined jointly by the Atomic Energy Commission and the Department of Defense; and that the necessary ordnance developments and carrier program be undertaken concurrently.

　　I have also decided to indicate publicly the intention of this Government to continue work to determine the feasibility of a thermonuclear weapon, and I hereby direct that no further official information be made public on it without my approval.

　　I am sending copies of this letter to the Secretary of State and the Secretary of Defense for their information.

Sincerely yours,

HARRY S. TRUMAN

OCT 9 1976

Honorable David Lilienthal
Chairman
Atomic Energy Commission
Washington

DECLASSIFIED
E. O. 11652, Sec. 3(E) and 5(D) or (E)
OSD letter, April 12, 1973
By NLT: _____ NARS Date 10-28-75

cc: The Secretary of State
　　The Secretary of Defense

TOP SECRET

of 500 Kilotons (500 thousand tons) and was anticlimactic. King was tested in case Mike didn't work and all those millions of dollars went to waste. King was the largest atomic bomb until that time. King meant kilotons and Mike meant megatons.

I remember that shortly afterward, reports began to appear in American newspapers from eyewitnesses to Mike. The Joint Chiefs of Staff sent an investigative team to find the sources of the leak. I encrypted the report, which took approximately eight hours and resulted in our being banned from talking about the operation for ten years.

46 I REMEMBER being only 21 years old and already having 450 flight hours.

I remember I never gave a thought about being 21 and being shot and killed.

I remember believing luck is the combination of preparation and opportunity. There is no such thing as luck.

I remember hobnobbing a bit in the British pubs, admiring the English for putting up with us. They'd say, "The Americans are overplayed, oversexed, and over here."

I remember preparing and waiting for D-Day, but not knowing what day it would be.

I remember I had 21 paratroopers. We took off and dropped behind the beaches south of Sainte-Mère-Église.

I remember counting 46 holes in my airplane.

I remember our crew receiving four cases of champagne "courtesy of General Patton."

I remember walking around Brussels after the Germans had left, and the children were throwing snowballs at us. We were throwing snowballs back. There we were in sheepskin jackets with .45's on our hips.

I remember getting a call that my beautiful, healthy baby girl had been born.

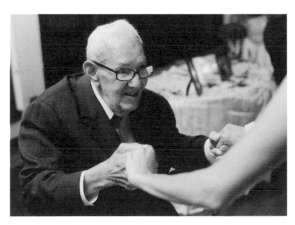

47 I REMEMBER being overwhelmed with fear as we set out in seven-ton vehicles on Route Michigan to help with Fallujah's first national elections. Our convoy carried ballots and antenna equipment for media outlets. Vehicle-borne improvised explosive devices were on the rise and a seven-ton could easily become a death trap. I remember I bowed my head, just as I did any time we convoyed, and I prayed, "Please God, just let me see my father one more time."

I remember before I could open my eyes and raise my head, there was a loud, rumbling explosion coming from the seven-ton behind us. It had blocked a bomb-laden taxi from ramming into me. The Marine passenger was fatally injured.

I remember seeing Iraqi soldiers play soccer with the bomber's bloated, decapitated head, which had landed 50 feet away.

I remember seeing the bomber's severed hand next to our vehicle and the rest of his torso feet away from me.

I remember the bright-red, bloodstained ground where my Marine friend lay as the corpsman tried to stop the bleeding. I now, and always will, have an overwhelming sense of guilt that is both a curse and a gift.

I remember it was truly the first time I'd ever felt loved.

I remember sitting in our wooden shack in Helmand province, Afghanistan. We had all returned from separate missions as combat correspondents.

I Remember:

One of my biggest fears as a leader was sending a junior Marine on a mission who doesn't return. I was thankful we were all alive, all together. We were eating Oreos and ramen noodles, and watching *Training Day*. Some of the best moments in my career, we were sitting, doing nothing. This is my heaven. If I died today, I'd want to return to this moment for eternity.

I remember my first reaction in combat was to grab my camera. Putting it up to my face gave me a sense of security and safety. But images I took are forever embedded in my mind. I see them every day, sometimes in my dreams.

I remember the last day of my military contract. I want the American public to know that I honestly tried to do my best to capture history with my camera and pen, and to inform them of what their Marines did in the toughest situations.

I remember the sadness I felt after I transferred to DePaul after serving twelve years as a Marine. It should've been a fun time, but I kept to myself. I didn't fit in. I had been through two wars and lost dozens of friends at the hands of brutal terrorists.

I remember we were all just kids. Now, I'm broken, struggling to smile each day, but at least I do. Mourn. Heal. Live.

48 I REMEMBER the jungled mountains southwest of the old imperial city of Huế. They were full of living things—leeches, centipedes, two kinds of mosquitoes, strange birds that cried during the day and strange animals that rustled at night.

I remember one June morning when Third Squad, doing a reconnaissance up a small stream, blundered into an impromptu ambush by a North Vietnamese Army rocket team. Casualties were "light"—only "Army" Armstrong, who was hit in the knee, and our Kit Carson scout, a 17-year-old ex-Viet Cong named Tuy, who died from loss of blood on the medevac chopper. The relief party that I was on shot one of the ambushers. He looked young, about the same age as Tuy and most of us. We stripped his rosette-pocked body, booby-trapped it and left in the stream. I still have a small, faded Kodacolor snapshot of Tuy. His cigarette dangles from his lips at the same slant as the M-16 rifle his right hand holds. Tough guy. But when I'd tried to speak Vietnamese to him, he smiled shyly.

For Vietnamese, death far from home—*chết đường*—is an unspeakable tragedy because their loved ones become wandering souls. In 2010 my Vietnamese wife and I hiked uphill through that same green forest where Tuy had been shot. The bird cries faded by mid morning. Her father had served alongside the Americans as a South Vietnamese Army lieutenant and had died young. Once, as a girl scavenging war metal in the forest, she'd found herself in a field of bones. That evening in Huế, during the Full Moon Festival, we strolled in the dusk past tiny leaping bonfires of offerings to the unhappy, still-wandering dead.

49 I REMEMBER attending church with my family on Veterans Day every year. I felt immense and gleaming pride when the congregation would applaud my father.

I remember September 11th. The entire build up to the war felt to me like a pissed off street brawler looking for someone to punch, no matter who it was. I remember as a Marine, we were trained "Not to ask why, but to do and die." Nevertheless, even my young 21-year-old mind smelled bullshit from the beginning.

I remember bringing shoes, candy, and soccer balls to some local children.

I remember their huge smiles because now they had an actual ball to kick instead of an empty plastic water bottle.

I remember the lump in my throat when I confirmed grid coordinates for a fire mission to air assets knowing it would end some of the lives of those same children.

I remember what I will never forget: the first time I heard a round hit someone. Not the report of the rifle, but the surprisingly loud snap of a bullet ripping through flesh and breaking bone.

I remember thinking just get through this patrol, this week, this month... just get home. Just get your men back to their families.

I remember wondering how in the hell I would ever explain a day in Iraq to anyone. Any little sound at night sends chills up and down my spine. I haven't touched a firearm since leaving the service, yet I still instinctively grab for one at night when nightmares wake me. My family asks me to get therapy. But the guilt I feel for my fallen friends is the only part of them I have left. The guilt of returning home when my friends didn't is only made worse by attempting to rid myself of that same guilt.

50 I REMEMBER the love. You probably have the wrong idea about war. War isn't about hate: it's about love. Hate has no place in war. You shoot at a person not because you hate him, or you hate his ideology, or because crazy ole Sergeant Hubble told you to. You do it because he's trying to kill somebody you love.

I remember Specialist Johnson after finding out ole Jodie got his girl and kid back home. "Jodies" are the guys back home who steal your girl when you head overseas. He got the dreaded phone call and it was bad. Jodie was living in his house, under his dollar. The tears came quick and hard. Nothing pulled from the pits of hell could have been as horrifying as the moments between his sobs.

I remember the rosy flares raining down from the helicopter as they saluted and I remember that damned song that played nearly every night over the loudspeaker as we sent another son home.

I remember loving each and every one of them.

I remember the guilt, but that's probably not a memory.

I remember the abrupt end to that love when we touched down back home. Everyone went their own ways. I miss that rocket city, because you won't find that kind of love anywhere else. //

Biographies

1

NAME: Brett Perry
WAR: Operation Enduring Freedom (Afghanistan)
BRANCH: Army
RANK: Staff Sergeant
PLATOON/BATTALION: Battle Company, 173rd Airborne Brigade
AGE AT ENLISTMENT: 21
SERVICE LENGTH: 2 years in Afghanistan and 7 years of service
ROLE: Infantry

2

NAME: Brian Quang Ngo
WAR: Afghanistan
BRANCH: Marine Corps
RANK: Corporal
PLATOON/BATTALION: 1st Combat Engineer Battalion
AGE AT ENLISTMENT: 20
SERVICE LENGTH: 8 Months
ROLE: Electrical Engineer: the implementation and maintenance of power generating equipment; providing electrical and utility support for frontline operation and remote areas.

3

NAME: Peter "Rabbit" Dodge
WAR: Vietnam
BRANCH: U.S. Army
RANK: E-5
PLATOON/BATTALION: 133 Medical Group, USARSUPTHAI
AGE AT ENLISTMENT: 23
SERVICE LENGTH: 1 year/3 years
ROLE: Preventive Medicine

4

NAME: Aaron Pylinski
WAR: Afghanistan 2002,
Iraq 2003–2004, Afghanistan 2007
BRANCH: U.S. Army
RANK: SSG
PLATOON/BATTALION: 3/505th
Parachute Infantry Regiment and
313th MI Battalion
AGE AT ENLISTMENT: 24 the first time
SERVICE LENGTH: 3 years, time in
service: 11 years, 8 months
ROLE: Intel Analyst, Squad Leader,
Platoon Sergeant, 82nd Airborne Division,
Intelligence Collection Manager

5

NAME: Michael "Red" Daniels
WAR: Operation Iraqi Freedom (OIF)
and Operation Enduring Freedom (OEF)
BRANCH: U.S. Army
RANK: E-5 (Sergeant)
PLATOON/BATTALION: Alpha Company
1st Platoon/27th Engineer Battalion
AGE AT ENLISTMENT: 20

SERVICE LENGTH: OIF: 8 months,
5 years real service; OEF: 12 months
ROLE: Airborne (Paratrooper),
Combat Engineer, Team Lead—
Machine Gun Team

6

NAME: Terrence Doyle
WAR: Iraq, Global War on Freedom
BRANCH: U.S. Navy
RANK: LEDR (Lieutenant Commander)
PLATOON/BATTALION:
Ship: USS Antietam Station
Comusnaucent CSTF-HOA
AGE AT ENLISTMENT: 23–24, 29–30, 33
SERVICE LENGTH: 18 months, 2 years,
1 year/13 years
ROLE: Auxiliaries Officer, Operations
Officer, Navigator, Ship's Officer,
Joint Planner, Training Officer,
Watchstander/Battle Watch Captain,
Somalia Unit LNO

7

NAME: Daniel "Bones" Hulsey
WAR: Operation Enduring Freedom
2010–2011
BRANCH: Army
RANK: Specialist
PLATOON/BATTALION:
1st Squadron 2nd Cavalry Regiment
Reconnaissance Platoon
AGE AT ENLISTMENT: 19
SERVICE LENGTH: 12 month deployment
length/3.5 years service length
ROLE: Driver, Senior Scout Observer,
Radio Transmitter Operator, Squad
Designated Marksman, Team Leader

8

NAME: Tom "Rocky" Nawrocki
WAR: Vietnam Era
BRANCH: USMC
RANK: Sgt.
PLATOON/BATTALION:
Marine Air Traffic Control Unit
AGE AT ENLISTMENT: 19
SERVICE LENGTH: 1966–1970
ROLE: Air Traffic Controller

9

NAME: Ben Vineyard (no nickname, except "dumb shit!" from my first sergeant)
WAR: European Theater, WW2
BRANCH: Field Artillery
RANK: proudly, corporal
PLATOON/BATTALION: forgotten, sorry
AGE AT ENLISTMENT: 19
SERVICE LENGTH: 3 years
ROLE: gunner, 105 mm howitzer

10

NAME: Susan M. Winstead
WAR: Persian Gulf War
BRANCH: U.S. Army
RANK: Captain
PLATOON/BATTALION: 17th Signal Battalion, 22nd Signal Brigade
AGE AT ENLISTMENT: 29
SERVICE LENGTH: I served in Germany from 1988 to 1993

ROLE: I was branched in the Signal Corp. I held positions of platoon leader, company executive officer, supply officer, adjutant, company commander, division staff officer, and readiness group.

11

NAME: Gordon "Stan" Stanley
WAR: Korea
BRANCH: U.S. Navy Rank: PN13
PLATOON/BATTALION: USS Piedmont
AGE AT ENLISTMENT: 20
SERVICE LENGTH: 2½ years
ROLE: In charge of the Engining Office

12

NAME: Joseph Kerke
WAR: Vietnam Era, non-combat
BRANCH: U.S. Marine Corps
RANK: Lieutenant Colonel
PLATOON/BATTALION: 80th Officer Candidate Course, Officer Candidate School, Quantico, VAE Company, Class 5-73, The Basic School, Quantico, VA Field Artillery Officer Basic Course, US Army Field Artillery School, Fort Sill, OK Battery B, 1st Battalion, 10th Marines, 2nd Marine Division FMF, Camp Lejeune, NC; deployed with Special Mission Force, GTMO; deployed with Battalion Landing Team 2/8, Landing Force 6th FleetBattery K, 4th Battalion, 14th Marines, 4th Marine Division FMF, USMCR, Joliet, IL Headquarters and Service Company, 2nd Battalion, 24th Marines, 4th Marine Division FMF, USMCR, Chicago, IL
AGE AT ENLISTMENT: 23
SERVICE LENGTH: Active duty: 3 years; Reserve: 36 years
ROLE: Billets held: 105mm (towed M101A) howitzer battery platoon commander; Artillery Liason Officer/ Battalion Fire Support Coordinator; 155mm (SP M109A1) howitzer battery Asst. Executive Officer; 1155mm (SP M109A1) howitzer battery commander

13
NAME: Robert "Bob" Zeman
WAR: Vietnam
BRANCH: US Navy
RANK: Seaman
PLATOON/BATTALION:
USS Theodore E Chandler DD717
AGE AT ENLISTMENT: 19
SERVICE LENGTH: deployed 1967/68;
service 1965/68
ROLE: VC1 NAS Barbers Point
Hawaii, Flight Ops Yeoman. At sea,
Boatwinmate: maintained ship,
steered by helm and lee helm, stood
watches, GQ forward magazine under
forward gun 6" 50's.

14
NAME: Rolando "Z" Zavala
WAR: Iraq (O.I.F. 07–09) Afghanistan
(O.E.F. 10–11)
BRANCH: U.S. Army
RANK: SSG/E-6

PLATOON/BATTALION:
A-BTRY 1/320th FAR 3rd Platoon
AGE AT ENLISTMENT: 22 in Iraq,
25 in Afghanistan
SERVICE LENGTH: 15 months in Iraq,
10 months in Afghanistan
ROLE: 13-Bravo Artillery Section Chief,
Squad Leader on deployment

15
NAME: Larry "The Bear" Grabowski
WAR: Vietnam
BRANCH: Army
RANK: SP5
PLATOON/BATTALION:
D Co, 4th Bn, 3rd Infantry, 11th Infantry
Bde, Americal Division
AGE AT ENLISTMENT: 23
SERVICE LENGTH: 6 months /22 months
ROLE: Infantry (11B10), Finance specialist

16
NAME: Gerald "Sgt. Goody" Goodman
WAR: Vietnam
BRANCH: Army
RANK: Staff Sergeant E-6
PLATOON/BATTALION:
Data Service Center
AGE AT ENLISTMENT: 20
SERVICE LENGTH: Vietnam 1 year/3 years,
9 months
ROLE: Processing unit information at
USARV Headquarters

17
NAME: Richard Johns
WAR: Vietnam
BRANCH: U.S. Army
RANK: SSgt
PLATOON/BATTALION: Co.A 1st Bn.
501st Airborne Inf. 101st Abn. Div.
AGE AT ENLISTMENT: 19
SERVICE LENGTH: 3 years in
U.S. Army, 1 year in Vietnam
ROLE: Infantryman, Paratrooper

18

NAME: Allen B. Chandler
WAR: Vietnam
BRANCH: Air Force
RANK: Retired as a Master Sergeant
PLATOON/BATTALION: In addition to these assignments in Vietnam: 315th Air Commando Wing, 19th Air Commando Squadron, Tan and 17th Special Operations Squadron (SOS), I served in 21 other countries during my Air Force career.
AGE AT ENLISTMENT: Joined the Air Force when I was 18. First time in Vietnam I was 22–23; second time I was 25.
SERVICE LENGTH: 21 years
ROLE: Worked on a variety of aircraft including Crew Chief on H19 helicopters, Crew chief on C-123s, Illuminator Operator on AC-119Gs.

19

NAME: Stanley E. Herzog
WAR: Vietnam
BRANCH: Army
RANK: Specialist 6
PLATOON/BATTALION: HHC 4th ID
AGE AT ENLISTMENT: 23
SERVICE LENGTH: 3 years/1 year in Vietnam
ROLE: Stenographer for BG Jack MacFarlane 4th ID ADC B in Vietnam, Stenographer for MG Ward Ryan 5th Army Headquarters Ft. Sheridan, IL

20

NAME: Chris K
WAR: Operation Iraqi Freedom, Operation Enduring Freedom
BRANCH: Air Force
RANK: Major
PLATOON/BATTALION: Multiple Flying Squadrons
AGE AT ENLISTMENT: 24–33
SERVICE LENGTH: 12 months of deployments/11 years service
ROLE: Air Force C-17 Pilot

21

NAME: Keilita Cuevas
WAR: Operation Iraqi Freedom
BRANCH: U.S. Army Active
RANK: Sergeant
PLATOON/BATTALION: Echo Battery 5/7 Air Defense Artillery—69th Brigade
AGE AT ENLISTMENT: 22
SERVICE LENGTH: 6 months/6.5 years
ROLE: PATRIOT Launching Station Enhanced Operator/Maintainer (14T)

22

NAME: Gilbert "Bogie" Elenbogen
WAR: WWII
BRANCH: Army Air Force
RANK: S/sgt
PLATOON/BATTALION:
AGE AT ENLISTMENT: 18
SERVICE LENGTH:
7 months/2 years/7 months
ROLE: Flight Engineer B-24

23

NAME: Michael R. Hammermeister
WAR: Vietnam Era
BRANCH: Army
RANK: SP4
PLATOON/BATTALION:
USARAL NCO Academy
AGE AT ENLISTMENT: 21
SERVICE LENGTH: 2 years
(January 1969–December 1970)
ROLE: Military Clerk Typist

24

NAME: Robert Gorman
WAR: Vietnam
BRANCH: Army
RANK: 1LT
PLATOON/BATTALION:
101st Airborne Division
AGE AT ENLISTMENT: 23
SERVICE LENGTH: 12 months
ROLE: Public Information Officer

25

NAME: Antoinette "Toni" Ellison
WAR: n/a
BRANCH: U.S. Navy
RANK: E-5
PLATOON/BATTALION: Duty Station
Commander Naval Fleet, Japan; Naval
Station, Diego Garcia; Naval Drug
Rehabilitation Center, San Diego, CA;
Naval Station, Guam
AGE AT ENLISTMENT: 24
SERVICE LENGTH: 8 years, 5 months
ROLE: Telecommunications Operator;
Substance Abuse Counselor

26

NAME: Robert "Ragman" Getz
WAR: Vietnam
BRANCH: Army, Infantry—Paratrooper
RANK: In Vietnam—
Captain Retired—Major
PLATOON/BATTALION: 1st Tour
Vietnam, Senior Advisor, 5th Railway
Security Battalion; 2nd Tour Vietnam,
Commander, Company Size Task
Force, 2ndBattalion, 503rd Infantry

Parachute Regiment, 173rd Airborne
Brigade (SEP)
AGE AT ENLISTMENT: 1st tour—24,
2nd tour—26
SERVICE LENGTH: Deployment—
two tours of twelve months length
for a total of 24 months equal to
4 overseas bars
ROLE: Training Officer, Advisor,
Commander, Logistics Officer

27

NAME: Shaakira Alexander
WAR: Operation Iraqi Freedom, 2003
BRANCH: Active Duty Army
RANK: Specialist
PLATOON/BATTALION: 2nd Platoon
551st Transportation Corps.
AGE AT ENLISTMENT: 18
SERVICE LENGTH: 3 years
ROLE: 88 Hotel, Cargo Specialist

28

NAME: Dennis K. Fallen
WAR: Vietnam, Operations Desert Storm and Desert Shield
BRANCH: USN— Retired
RANK: Seaman through Petty Officer 2nd Class, Retired Rank— Lieutenant Commander
PLATOON/BATTALION: VP-60, NAS Glenview; Naval Hospital Bethesda, Uniformed Services University of the Health Sciences, Naval Hospital Great Lakes
AGE AT ENLISTMENT: 19 Vietnam, 38 Operation Desert Storm
SERVICE LENGTH: Anti-submarine Patrol Squadron—Personnelman: 4 years active duty, 4 year active reserve; Medical Service Corps Officer—Healthcare Administrator/ Medical Intelligence: 15 years reserve, 1 year active duty
ROLE: Enlisted service: Personnelman in an Aviation Squadron with other flight observer responsibilities. Officer service: During Operation Desert Storm/Shield, served as a Hospital Administrator National Naval Medical Center Bethesda as Director of Administration for the Medical Directorate and later as special legislative aide to the Navy Surgeon General. Reserve Duty: Unit Administrative and Executive Officer, Adjunct Faculty at the Uniformed Services University of the Health Sciences in the Department of Military Medicine.

29

NAME: Meosha "Mo" Thomas
WAR: Global War on Terrorism/ Operation Iraqi Freedom
BRANCH: United States Navy
RANK: E5
PLATOON/BATTALION: N/A
AGE AT ENLISTMENT: 18
SERVICE LENGTH: 10 years
ROLE: As an Information Systems Technician Petty Officer Second Class Surface Warfare (IT2 SW), I maintained the Navy's global satellite telecommunications systems, mainframe computers, local and wide area networks, and micro-computer systems used in the fleet.

30

NAME: Brian E Berndt
WAR: Iraq
BRANCH: National Guard
RANK: SPC
PLATOON/BATTALION: Maintenance
AGE AT ENLISTMENT: 23
SERVICE LENGTH: 18 months
ROLE: Mechanic, Truck Driver, Fueler

31

NAME: Matt Pierson
WAR: Operation Enduring Freedom ('04–'05), Operation Iraqi Freedom ('05–'06)
BRANCH: US Marine Corps
RANK: Captain
PLATOON/BATTALION: 2nd Platoon, India Company, 3 Battalion 6th Marines (unit while in Afghanistan/Iraq)
AGE AT ENLISTMENT: 24 and 25
SERVICE LENGTH: 7 months in Afghanistan, 7 months in Iraq; 6 years on active duty
ROLE: Infantry Platoon Commander, Officer-in-Charge (for training mission in the Republic of Georgia), Reconnaissance Platoon Commander, Force Recon Platoon Commander

32

NAME: Fred Woods
WAR: Iraq
BRANCH: USCG
RANK: E-6
PLATOON/BATTALION:
AGE AT ENLISTMENT: 26
SERVICE LENGTH: 13 months in country, 10 years total
ROLE: Law enforcement, search and rescue

33

NAME: Henry "Hank" Silva Jr.
WAR: Vietnam (Cold)
BRANCH: United States Air Force
RANK: E7 Master Sargent
PLATOON/BATTALION: 1974 Communications Computer Group
AGE AT ENLISTMENT: 20
SERVICE LENGTH: 20 years, 6 months
ROLE: Computer Operations, Metrologist/Precision Measuring Equipment Specialist

34

NAME: Elaine Little
WAR: They called us "peacekeepers in Bosnia." I was in Afghanistan from 2004–2005.
BRANCH: Army
RANK: From PFC to Warrant Officer 2
PLATOON/BATTALION: 341st MI BN in Chicago (National Guard) was the last one
AGE AT ENLISTMENT: 46
SERVICE LENGTH: 15 Months
ROLE: Interrogator in Afghanistan, broadcast journalist in Bosnia, many others to include Psychological Operations Specialist, Russian linguist, Morse code interceptor, and motion picture specialist

35

NAME: John "Jack" Summers
WAR: WWII (1942–1946)
BRANCH: U.S. Navy
RANK: Y2C (Yeoman)
PLATOON/BATTALION:
Originally Navy Pier, Chicago, IL
Legal Dept.
AGE AT ENLISTMENT: 19
SERVICE LENGTH: 4 years (last two years Guam, Naval Base)
ROLE: One year Navy Pier, Chicago, IL; NOB, Navy Operation Base Aquana, Guam; One semester, Dartmouth College, N.H.

36

NAME: Donna L. Cooper
WAR: Iraq
BRANCH: Army—Illinois Army National Guard
RANK: Colonel (Ret) Rank At Deployment Major
PLATOON/BATTALION: Assigned to STARC State Area Command ARNG FWD 1301 N. MacArthur Blvd.

Springfield, IL for Deployment from HHC, 33rd Area Support Group, 1551 N. Kedzie Ave. Chicago, IL 60651
AGE AT ENLISTMENT: 50
SERVICE LENGTH: In country 11 Months, 20 days. Entered active duty, 17 August 2003, separated 24 August 2004.
ROLE: State Command Judge Advocate, April 2012 to February 2013; Command Staff Judge Advocate, 108th Sustainment Brigade (2005–2012) and 404th Chemical Brigade September 2004–2005; Assistant Staff Judge Advocate, 33rd ASG and 33rd SIB 1993–2003 Jobs while deployed: Deputy Chief Legal Advisor and Liaison Officer; MND (C-S) [MND-multinational division- central south]; US Army General Staff; CJTF-7 from August 2003 to January 2004; Chief Legal Advisor and Liaison Officer from January 2004 to July 2004; Foreign Claims Commission; Certifying Officer 24 December 2003 to June 2004

37

NAME: Karina "Sergeant Smiley" Lopez
WAR: First Deployment: Operation Enduring Freedom 10–11; Second Deployment: Operation Enduring Freedom 14
BRANCH: United States Army Reserves
RANK: Sergeant
PLATOON/BATTALION:
First Deployment: Deployable Command Post (DCP) 2/416th Theater Engineer Command; Second Deployment: Aegis Platoon/300th Human Resources Company
AGE AT ENLISTMENT:
First Deployment: 20, Second Deployment: 24
SERVICE LENGTH: First Deployment: 10 months; Second Deployment: 6 months; In the service now 6 years and still counting
ROLE: First Deployment: Human Resources Specialist for Joint Engineer Command; Second Deployment: Postal Operations and Rodeo Sergeant

38

NAME: Connie "Meach" Meacham (at time of service). I married in Frankfort Germany and became Connie Craig for my last 9 months in the service.
WAR: Vietnam Era
BRANCH: USAF
RANK: Sergeant
PLATOON/BATTALION: Strategic Air Command
AGE AT ENLISTMENT: 18 when I joined the USAF
SERVICE LENGTH: 4.5 years
ROLE: Ground-to-air radio operations

39

NAME: Randall "Randy Racoon" Rollinson
WAR: Vietnam
BRANCH: Army
RANK: E5
PLATOON/BATTALION: HQ USARV
AGE AT ENLISTMENT: 20
SERVICE LENGTH: 1 year
ROLE: Primarily, administrative

40

NAME: Mark Ludeking
WAR: Operation Enduring Freedom
BRANCH: United States Army
RANK: CPT
PLATOON/BATTALION: 633rd Theater Gateway
AGE AT ENLISTMENT: 26
SERVICE LENGTH: 9 months
ROLE: Operations Officer

41

NAME: Msgt. Steven M. Kraslen
WAR: Vietnam
BRANCH: USAF
RANK: E-4 at the time
PLATOON/BATTALION: 15th Aerial Port Squadron
AGE AT ENLISTMENT: 20
SERVICE LENGTH: 12 Months
ROLE: Load and off-load Cargo Transport Aircraft; inspected cargo pallets before being shipped back to the USA; set up cargo loads for outgoing aircraft; spent some time on TDYs to other bases for special cargo moves supporting campaigns

42

NAME: Sandra Webb-Booker
WAR: Bosnia
BRANCH: US Army
RANK: MAJ while in Bosnia
PLATOON/BATTALION: Civil Affairs
AGE AT ENLISTMENT: 47
SERVICE LENGTH: 9 months/service length 28 years
ROLE: Combat support Hospital (CSH) Officer in Charge of the Surgical Intensive Care; Civil Affairs Public Health Nurse; CGSOC Instructor; Commander 801st CSH, Fort Sheridan; Chief Nurse, 330th Medical BDE

43

NAME: Doug "Flash" Nielsen
WAR: Vietnam
BRANCH: USMC
RANK: PFC Platoon/Battalion: HQ, 2nd Btn, 12 Marines, 3rd Marine Division
AGE AT ENLISTMENT: 19
SERVICE LENGTH: In country 11½ months
ROLE: 2511, Wireman

44
NAME: Ned B. Ricks
WAR: Vietnam
BRANCH: U.S. Army
RANK: At the time of Vietnam service, I was a captain; retired as a major.
PLATOON/BATTALION: In Vietnam, I served in the 1st (Air) Squadron, 9th Cavalry, 1st Cavalry Division (Airmobile). I was also Commanding Officer of Troop C, 1st Squadron, 10th Cavalry, First Field Forces Vietnam.
AGE AT ENLISTMENT: When I went to Vietnam in 1970, I was a young 23 years old. I returned home age 24 (going on 60).
SERVICE LENGTH: My tour of duty in Vietnam was from July 1970 to July 1971. I served in the Regular Army from 1968 to 1975 and the US Army Reserves until 1993, a total of 25 years commissioned service.
ROLE: armored cavalry platoon leader; aide de camp to a general officer; squadron (same size as battalion) operations officer; squadron adjutant; armored cavalry troop commander (same size as a company); brigade adjutant; headquarters company commander; brigade operations officer; theater army level logistics headquarters commander; military intelligence detachment commander; theater army headquarters level assistant inspector general

45
NAME: Roger Loeffler
WAR: Korea
BRANCH: Army
RANK: Cpl.
PLATOON/BATTALION: 7132 AU
AGE AT ENLISTMENT: 20
SERVICE LENGTH: 2 years
ROLE: Cryptographer

46
NAME: Philip Hecker
WAR: WWII
BRANCH: Army (Air Corps)
RANK: O3 Captain
PLATOON/BATTALION:
AGE AT ENLISTMENT: 20
SERVICE LENGTH: 1942–1946
ROLE: C-47 Captain, dropped paratroopers; served during D-Day, dropped men and supplies over France

47
NAME: Heidi Agostini
WAR: Operation Iraqi Freedom, Operation Enduring Freedom
BRANCH: Marines Rank: E-6/staff sergeant
PLATOON/BATTALION: I Marine Expeditionary Force
AGE AT ENLISTMENT: 23
SERVICE LENGTH: both 7 months
ROLE: Served as a combat correspondent, producing articles, videos and photography to tell the Marines' story both in combat and stateside.

48

NAME: Jim Fairhall
WAR: Vietnam
BRANCH: Army
RANK: SP-4
PLATOON/BATTALION:
Alpha Company, 1/502d Infantry
Brigade, 101st Airborne Division
AGE AT ENLISTMENT: 22
SERVICE LENGTH: 13.5 months
ROLE: Infantry

49

NAME: Patrick "Rock Star" Cochrun
WAR: Iraq 2003–2004
BRANCH: USMC
RANK: Sgt.
PLATOON/BATTALION: 3/24
AGE AT ENLISTMENT: 23–34
SERVICE LENGTH: 7 months each time
ROLE: Infantry

50

NAME: Mike Parker
WAR: Afghanistan
BRANCH: U.S. Army
RANK: SGT
PLATOON/BATTALION:
125th BSB/3/1 AD
AGE AT ENLISTMENT: 21
SERVICE LENGTH: 1 year deployment,
4 years active, currently serving
4 more in reserves
ROLE: Intel Analyst

Photographs

COVER
Chicago Flag, Viet Nam, 1971
by Laszlo Kondor

PAGE 11
courtesy of Jim Fairhall (48)

PAGE 16
courtesy of Doug Nielsen (43)

PAGE 17
Brett Perry (1) by Jasmine Clark

PAGE 18
Brian Ngo (2) by Jasmine Clark

PAGE 20, left to right
Aaron Pylinski (4) by Jasmine Clark
courtesy of Aaron Pylinski (4)

PAGE 22
courtesy of Elaine Little (34)

PAGE 25
courtesy of Rolando Zavala (14)

PAGES 28–29
courtesy of Tom Nawrocki (8)

PAGE 32
courtesy of Susan Winstead (10)

PAGE 33
courtesy of Gordon Stanley (11)

PAGE 34
courtesy of Rolando Zavala (14)

PAGE 35
courtesy of Robert Zeman (13)

PAGE 37
courtesy of Allen Chandler (18)

PAGE 39
The Vietnam Veterans Memorial in Washington, D.C., U.S. Navy photo by Photographer's Mate 2nd Class Daniel J. McLain

PAGES 40, 41
courtesy of Stanley Herzog (19)

PAGE 43
courtesy of Keilita Cuevas (21)

PAGE 44
courtesy of Gilbert Elenbogen (22)

PAGE 48
courtesy of Robert Getz (26)

PAGE 50
courtesy of Meosha Thomas (29)

PAGE 52
courtesy of Matt Pierson (31)

PAGE 55
courtesy of Henry Silva Jr. (33)

PAGE 57
three photos courtesy of Elaine Little (34)

PAGES 58, 59
courtesy of John Summers (35)

PAGE 60
courtesy of Karina Lopez (37)

PAGE 61
courtesy of Connie Meacham (38)

PAGE 62
Sandra Webb-Booker (42) by Jasmine Clark

PAGE 63
courtesy of Doug Nielsen (43)

PAGE 64
two photos courtesy of Ned Ricks (44)

PAGE 67
two photos courtesy of Roger Loeffler (45)

PAGE 69
three photos courtesy of Philip Hecker (46)

PAGE 70
courtesy of Heidi Agostini (47)

PAGE 73
Tuy, 1970, courtesy of Jim Fairhall (48)

PAGE 74
courtesy of Patrick Cochrun (49)

Acknowledgments

// **THE BOOK WAS MANAGED** in its various phases by undergraduate and graduate students in the DePaul English Department's Big Shoulders Books three course sequence in publishing. The following students in Pre-Production, Production, and Post-Production all worked as collaborative storytellers to make this book a reality: Maria Babich, Rachel Bean, Ryan Bowton, Phillip Brumbaugh, Steffan Carlson, Olivia Clarkin, Alma Cohen, Kimberly Keyworth, Alexander Cumming, Rachel Deahl, Jen DePoorter, Lorna Diaz, Amy Finn, Jonathan Garcia, Alexandra Gerard, Julia Getts, Molly Graham, Melinda Gray, Jacob Hall, Maximillian Hanak, Brittany Hamilton, Eric Hollander, Amanda Lawton, Timothy McDermott, Alexandra Messina-Schultheis, Taylor Morony, Katelyn O'Brien, Sara Ocytko, Samantha Okrasinski, Caitlyn Pagenkopf, Rachel Plotkin, Rachel Pomeroy, Caitlin Raleigh, Anastasia Sasewich, Sarah Tassoni, Michael Torpy, Sarah Williams, and Gabriella Zeller.

Of these students, I would like to acknowledge the exceptional efforts of **Melinda Gray**, **Alex Gerard**, **Taylor Morony**, **Rachel Plotkin**, **Sarah Williams**, and **Kim Keyworth**. They were profoundly helpful shaping this book, and Taylor and Kim were especially helpful finding veterans to participate. Also, I would like to thank **Colleen O'Connor** for her help as the instructor for the Production class. And I'd like to thank **Dana Kaye** for her expertise in promoting the book and her instruction of the Post-Production course.

I Remember: Chicago Veterans of War is the third book from Big Shoulders Press, a new press from DePaul University's English Department that aims to feature members of the Chicago community that need a voice. We give all copies away for free and try to distribute them as widely as possible. We've given away over 20,000 copies of our first book, *How Long Will I Cry? Voices of Youth Violence*. **Miles Harvey**, the editor of *How Long Will I Cry*, was an inspiration for this book—also, his assistance throughout this project was invaluable. Thank you to **Michele Morano** for her guidance in the planning stage of *I Remember*. I would also like to thank **Dave Welch**, the Managing Editor of Big Shoulders, for his tremendous help throughout the making of this book.

And of course, this book and Big Shoulders Books would not exist without the funding and enduring support by **Irene and Bill Beck**. Profound thanks to them for their belief and vital help.

I would also like to thank **Jasmine Clark**. She took photographic portraits of many of the veterans featured in these pages. She is an incredibly talented young photographer. Her efforts greatly enhanced the experience for the veterans featured here as well as the quality of this anthology.

Lastly, I want to offer special thanks to **Natalie Bontumasi**, the designer of this book. Her creativity, patience, and perseverance transformed *I Remember* into a visual piece of art. No one deserves more credit than Natalie for bringing this idea to life.

Veteran Resources

// **IF THESE STORIES** have resonated with you as a veteran, family member, or private citizen, then explore the organizations and resources below and consider your next step.

The Coalition of Veterans Organization
coalitionofvets.org

The Coalition of Veterans Organization is a group of individuals and member organizations whose purpose is to advocate and educate veterans and the public on issues that impact veterans and their families.

National Call Center for Homeless Veterans
877-4AIDVET (877-424-3838)
va.gov/homeless/nationalcallcenter.asp

The hotline is intended to assist homeless veterans and their families, VA Medical Centers, federal, state and local partners, community agencies, service providers, and others in the community.

Illinois Joining Forces
illinoisjoiningforces.org

Illinois Joining Forces (IJF) is a statewide, public-private network of veteran- and military-serving organizations.

Military with PTSD
militarywithptsd.org

Military with PTSD is a federal 501c3 tax-exempt organization dedicated to helping educate veterans, caretakers, and civilians about the effects of post-traumatic stress disorder (PTSD) on the veterans, in the family, and on the community as a whole. We help to improve and protect the lives of people livingwith PTSD.

Wounded Warrior Project
woundedwarriorproject.org

The Wounded Warrior Project's mission is to foster the most successful, well-adjusted generation of wounded service members in our nation's history.

Illinois Department of Veterans Affairs
illinois.gov

The mission of the Illinois Department of Veterans' Affairs (IDVA) is to empower veterans and their families to thrive.

About the Creative Team

CHRIS GREEN (Editor)
Chris Green is the author of three books of poetry: *The Sky Over Walgreens*, *Epiphany School*, and *Résumé*. His poetry has appeared in such publications as *Poetry*, *The New York Times*, *New Letters*, *Verse*, and *Nimrod*. He's edited four anthologies, including *Brute Neighbors: Urban Nature Poetry, Prose & Photography*. He teaches in the English Department at DePaul University. More information can be found at **www.chrisgreenpoetry.com**.

NATALIE MILLS BONTUMASI (Book Designer)
Natalie Mills Bontumasi has been a graphic designer in Chicago for over twenty years. Her company, Good Thomas Design, focuses on visual communication for non-profit organizations and small businesses. Her work is included in the Chicago Design Archive.

JIM FAIRHALL (Foreword)
Born in Greenwich Village, New York City, Jim Fairhall grew up in New York and England. He served as an infantryman in the 101st Airborne Division in Vietnam from March 1970 through April 1971. An English professor at DePaul University, Fairhall has written an award-winning book on James Joyce and history and is working on a book on Joyce and nature. He has also won national awards for his Vietnam-related creative writing— stories, a memoir-essay, and a poetry collection.

JASMINE CLARK (Photographer)
Jasmine Rayna Clark is the daughter of two United States Marines and grew up in a military community in Twentynine Palms, California (MCAGCC). Clark received her BFA in Photography from California State University, Long Beach and will receive her MFA in Photography from Columbia College Chicago in 2016. Her career in photography began with a long-term interest in the military, depictions and theories surrounding war photography, and the military's impact on the American landscape. Clark's current work focuses on the display of symbols of American patriotism, nationalism, religious belief, and support for the military in American landscapes.

LASZLO KONDOR (Cover Photographer)
Born in Hungary in 1940, Laszlo Kondor had a long career in photography. From 1970 to 1972, he served as combat photographer for the United States Army and later for the Department of Army's Special Photographic Office. He was also the official photographer for Chicago Mayor Richard J. Daley from 1972 to 1976. Kondor occasionally presented exhibits of his works, such as the 1995 exhibit "Vietnam: 20 Years Later, A Combat Photographer Remembers."